For over a decade, The New York Public Library and Oxford University Press have annually invited a prominent figure in the arts and letters to give a series of lectures on a topic of his or her choice. Subsequently these lectures become the basis of a book jointly published by the Library and the Press. For 2002 and 2003 the two institutions asked seven noted writers, scholars, and critics to offer a "meditation on temptation" on one of the seven deadly sins. *Gluttony* by Francine Prose is the second book from this lecture series.

Previous books from The New York Public Library/Oxford University Press Lectures are:

The Old World's New World by C. Vann Woodward
Culture of Complaint: The Fraying of America by Robert Hughes
Witches and Jesuits: Shakespeare's Macbeth by Garry Wills
Visions of the Future: The Distant Past, Yesterday, Today, Tomorrow
by Robert Heilbroner
Doing Documentary Work by Robert Coles
The Sun, the Genome, and the Internet by Freeman J. Dyson
The Look of Architecture by Witold Rybczynski
Visions of Utopia by Edward Rothstein, Herbert Muschamp,
and Martin E. Marty

Also by Francine Prose

Fiction

Blue Angel
Guided Tours of Hell
The Peaceable Kingdom
Primitive People
Women and Children First
Bigfoot Dreams
Hungry Hearts
Household Saints
Animal Magnetism
Marie Laveau
The Glorious Ones
Judah the Pious

Nonfiction

Sicilian Odyssey
The Lives of the Muses

Books for Young Adults and Children

After
The Angels' Mistake
The Demons' Mistake
You Never Know
The Dybbuk

Translations

A Scrap of Time
Traces
The Journey

Gluttony

The Seven Deadly Sins

Francine Prose

The New York Public Library

OXFORD
UNIVERSITY PRESS

OXFORD
UNIVERSITY PRESS

Oxford University Press, Inc., publishes works that
further Oxford University's objective of excellence
in research, scholarship, and education.

Oxford   New York
Auckland   Cape Town   Dar es Salaam   Hong Kong   Karachi
Kuala Lumpur   Madrid   Melbourne   Mexico City   Nairobi
New Delhi   Shanghai   Taipei   Toronto

With offices in
Argentina   Austria   Brazil   Chile   Czech Republic   France   Greece
Guatemala   Hungary   Italy   Japan   Poland   Portugal   Singapore
South Korea   Switzerland   Thailand   Turkey   Ukraine   Vietnam

First published by Oxford University Press, Inc., 2003
198 Madison Avenue, New York, NY 10016
www.oup.com

First issued as an Oxford University Press paperback, 2006
ISBN-13: 978-0-19-531205-8
ISBN-10: 0-19-531205-8

Oxford is a registered trademark of Oxford University Press

The Library of Congress has cataloged the hardcover edition as follows:
Prose, Francine, 1947–
Gluttony : the seven deadly sins / Francine Prose
p. cm.
Based on a lecture series in the humanities hosted by the New York Public Library.
Includes bibliographical references.
ISBN 0–19–515699–4
1. Gluttony. I. Title.
BV4627.G5P76 2003
178—dc21   2003042045

Book design by planettheo.com

9 8 7 6 5 4 3 2 1

Printed in the United States of America
on acid-free paper

Contents

Editor's Note

This volume is part of a lecture and book series on the Seven Deadly Sins cosponsored by The New York Public Library and Oxford University Press. Our purpose was to invite scholars and writers to chart the ways we have approached and understood evil, one deadly sin at a time. Through both historical and contemporary explorations, each writer finds the conceptual and practical challenges that a deadly sin poses to spirituality, ethics, and everyday life.

The notion of the Seven Deadly Sins did not originate in the Bible. Sources identify early lists of transgressions classified in the 4th century by Evagrius of Pontus and then by John of Cassius. In the 6th century, Gregory the Great formulated the traditional seven. The sins were ranked by increasing severity and judged to be the greatest offenses to the soul and the root of all other sins. As certain sins were subsumed into others and similar terms were used interchangeably according to theological review, the list evolved to include the seven as we know them: Pride, Greed, Lust, Envy, Gluttony, Anger, and Sloth. To counter these violations, Christian theologians classified the Seven Heavenly Virtues—the cardinal: Prudence, Temperance, Justice, Fortitude, and the theological: Faith, Hope, and Charity. The sins inspired medieval and Renaissance writers including Chaucer, Dante, and Spenser, who personified the seven in rich and memorable characters. Depictions grew to include associated colors, animals, and punishments in hell for the deadly offenses. Through history, the famous list has emerged in theological and philosophical tracts, psychology, politics, social criticism, popular culture, and art and literature. Whether the deadly seven to you represent the most common human foibles or more serious spiritual shortcomings, they stir the imagination and evoke the inevitable question— what is *your* deadly sin?

Our contemporary fascination with these age-old sins, our struggle against, or celebration of, them, reveals as much about our continued desire to define human nature as it does about our divine aspirations. I hope that this book and its companions invite the reader to indulge in a similar reflection on vice, virtue, the spiritual, and the human.

Elda Rotor

Gluttony

Introduction

Several years ago, I was invited to a midtown Manhattan restaurant for a lunch that was part of an ongoing series of gatherings hosted by two women who were writing a book about women's attitudes toward their bodies, eating, diet, weight loss, and so forth. The lunches were designed to enable the writers to talk to groups of women, to hear what women were saying about what they ate and what they didn't eat and how they felt about it—and to pick up clever dieting tips that readers might find useful.

Perhaps a dozen women attended. Some were plump, some were thin, all were attractive and appealing, none was anywhere near obese. But many of them described their relationship with food as a ferocious, lifelong battle for power and control.

The lines were drawn, the stakes were clear. In one corner was the women's resolve, their fragile self-regard, their sense of how they wanted to look and feel, how they wanted the world to see them; in the other corner was the refrigerator and a gallon of chocolate ice cream. One woman described how triumphant she felt when she succeeded in getting her carton of takeout dinner from the store all the way to her house without wolfing it down in the car on the drive home. Another passed along the helpful calorie-counting traveler's trick of calling ahead and asking the hotel at which she would be staying to please empty the mini-bar before she even checked in.

Unsurprisingly, the actual ordering of the lunch was fraught with watchfulness, self-consciousness, and more than a little tension. Decisions were made, minds were changed, requests rethought and altered. How much courage it took simply to ask for the crème brûlée. I can't remember precisely what I ate—it seems to me that everyone started with the salad—but what I do recall is suppressing an impulse to order two desserts just to see what would happen.

It's hard to imagine a similar event occurring in any century besides our own. It seems so quintessentially modern, so current and of the moment. What would Thomas Aquinas or Saint Augustine have made of that lunch, or, for that matter, of a world in which women called ahead with directives concerning the mini-bar contents? And yet, had the event taken place a thousand years in the past—let's say, at an early church council or synod—it would more likely have been recognized for what it really was, as something more substantial than a casual chat about body image and diet. Because in fact, it was a sort of metaphysical discussion, a forum on matters of the body and the spirit. For what were these women talking about except sin and virtue, abstinence, self-control, and the daunting challenge of overcoming the fierce temptations of gluttony?

Of all the seven deadly sins, gluttony has had perhaps the most intriguing and paradoxical history. The ways in which the sin has been viewed have evolved in accordance with the changing obsessions of society and culture. From the early Middle Ages until the early Renaissance, centuries during which mass consciousness was formed and dominated by the tenets of Christianity, the principal danger of gluttony was thought to reside in its nature as a form of idolatry, the most literal sort of navel gazing, of worshiping the belly as a God: a cult with rituals and demands that would inevitably divert and distract the faithful from true, authentic religion.

As the Renaissance and later the Industrial Revolution and eighteenth-century rationalism refocused the popular imagination from heaven to earth and adjusted the goals of labor to include the rewards of this world as well as those of the next, gluttony lost some of its stigma and eventually became almost a badge of pride. Substance, weight, and the ability to afford the most lavish pleasures of the table became visible signs of vitality, prosperity, and of the worldly success to which both the captains and the humble foot soldiers of industry were encouraged to aspire. At the same time, growing concerns (fostered by early writers on health and science) with health and longevity and with keeping the body in some sort of harmonious balance led to an increased interest in diet, moderation, and nutrition.

In the past few decades, as changing notions of physical attractiveness and desirability required that women (and to a somewhat lesser extent, men) be trim and thin, the dictates of beauty culture made gluttony appear as yet another sort of threat. Most recently, our fixation on health, our quasi-obscene fascination with illness and death, and our fond, impossible hope that diet and exercise will enable us to live forever have demonized eating in general and overeating in particular. Health consciousness and a culture fixated on death have transformed gluttony from a sin that leads to other sins into an illness that leads to other illnesses.

These days, few people seriously consider the idea that eating too much or enjoying one's food is a crime against God, a profound moral failure for which we will be promptly dispatched to hell. It's doubtful that even the most devoutly religious are likely to confess and seek absolution for looking forward to breakfast, or having taken pleasure in the delights of last night's dinner.

Yet even as gluttony has (at least in the popular imagination) ceased to be a spiritual transgression, food, the regulation of eating, and the related subjects of dieting, obesity, nutrition, etc., have become major cultural preoccupations. A casual survey of the self-help section of the local bookstore will make it clear how large a place gluttony (in its new, deconsecrated form) now occupies in our collective consciousness. For every volume offering advice about the contemporary equivalents of the other sins (sexual addiction, anger management, and so forth) there are dozens of books designed to help the hapless or self-loathing glutton (itself a notably unfashionable term) to repent and reform.

Meanwhile, the punishments suffered by the modern glutton are at once more complex and subtle than eternal damnation. Now that gluttony has become an affront to prevailing standards of beauty and health rather than an offense against God, the wages of sin have changed and now involve a version of hell on earth: the pity, contempt, and distaste of one's fellow mortals. What makes the glutton's penance all the more public and cruel is that gluttony is the only sin whose effects (in the absence of that rare and fortunate metabolism that permits the fruits of sin to remain hidden) are visible, written on the body. Unlike, say, the slothful, who can, if they wish, manage to appear alert and awake, the modern glutton pays for—and displays—transgression by violating the esthetic norms of a society that places an extreme and even potentially dangerous emphasis on fitness and thinness. In some cases, the punishment for the sin can be nearly as extreme as any suffered by those condemned to eternal damnation. Not long ago, a popular singer arranged to have her stomach stapled—a radical cure for gluttony—in an operation that was broadcast over the internet and could be watched as a kind of punitive mass entertainment.

To trace the evolution of gluttony is to consider where we have come from, where we have arrived, and where we may be heading. For if, as they say, we are what we eat, then how we feel about eating—and eating too much—reveals our deepest beliefs about who we are, what we will become, and about the connections and conflicts between the needs of the body and the hungers of the spirit.

CHAPTER ONE

Is Gluttony a Sin?

Too soon, too delicately, too expensively, too greedily, too much. Those are the five ways in which, according to Gregory the Great—the pioneer enumerator of the seven deadly sins—gluttony reveals itself or, alternately, hides, baiting its trap with the extra portion, the costly delicacy, the tempting between-meals snack.

> Sometimes it forestalls the hour of need; sometimes it seeks costly meats; sometimes it requires that food be daintily cooked; sometimes it exceeds the measure of refreshment by taking too much; sometimes we sin by the very heat of an immoderate appetite.[1]

In fact, Gregory's formulation describes the ways in which most of us eat, or think about eating, or plan to eat—on a more or less daily basis. Of the five warning signs that the sixth-century pope identified as the hallmarks of the sinner, there are really only two—"too greedily" and "too much"—that we continue to associate with gluttony. Does the desire for costly meats or dainty cooking really sound like a crime against God, an evil that should rightly consign us to spend eternity in the third circle of hell? If gluttony is indeed a sin, who among us is not guilty?

Like lust, its sister transgression, the sin of gluttony reflects a constellation of complex attitudes toward the confluence of necessity and pleasure. Unlike the other deadly sins, lust and gluttony are allied with behaviors required for the survival of the individual and the species. One has to eat in order to live; presumably, the race would die out if lust were never permitted to work its magic. And religion has no choice but to acknowledge and accept these self-evident realities.

Because hunger and sexual desire are essential human instincts, even the church fathers—those tireless warriors against the stirrings of biological impulse—were obliged to recognize that lust and gluttony could not be addressed and combated in quite the same ways in which the faithful were advised to struggle against the demons of pride, envy, greed. Sagely, the fourth-century monastic theologian John Cassian referred to these natural proclivities, gluttony and lust, as illnesses that require complex cures.

The traditional solution to the problems of gluttony and lust has been to suggest that the element of sin enters in only when we allow ourselves to relax and *enjoy* satisfying the needs of the body. We are allowed to eat and have sex as long as we don't *like* it. Just as the challenge facing the true believer is to be fruitful and multiply without experiencing lust, so it should be possible to eat without savoring our food. So the notion of gluttony considers the limit of what we need to survive and attempts to disassociate the minimum daily caloric requirement from the contaminating influences of craving, obsession, or pleasure. For both lust and gluttony are less a matter of act than of motive, less of content than of desire, less of impulse than of compulsion.

The fourth-century Desert Father, Evagrius of Pontus—a man whose ascetic regimen in the wilderness was at once a protest against the sin of gluttony and an occasion to spend a considerable amount of time contemplating its nature—has given us perhaps the most comprehensive definition of the sin, not nearly as logical and systematic as Gregory the Great's, but much more lyrical and thrilling:

> Gluttony is the mother of lust, the nourishment of evil thoughts,
> laziness in fasting, obstacle to asceticism, terror to moral purpose,
> the imagining of food, sketcher of seasonings, unrestrained colt,

unbridled frenzy, receptacle of disease, envy of health, obstruction of the (bodily) passages, groaning of the bowels, the extreme of outrages, confederate of lust, pollution of the intellect, weakness of the body, difficult sleep, gloomy death."[2]

Over the centuries, the seriousness, the centrality, the very nature of the sin changed as Judeo-Christian culture underwent a sharpening and an intensification of its innate and essential suspicions about the pleasures of the body. Only in its most recent incarnation (the contemporary horror of overweight, fat, and flesh itself) has the sin of gluttony been neatly separated from most associations with any idea of delight.

Only during the last few decades has the legacy of Puritanism (operating in close partnership with the interests of capitalism) deftly lifted desire and gratification out of the equation, and replaced the notion that humans might *like* eating with the suggestion that we eat principally out of compulsion, illness, self-destructiveness, the desire for self-obliteration, to avoid intimacy and social contact, and so forth. As our cultural concerns have shifted from a focus on religion, God, and the afterlife to an obsession with health and (by extension) the fantasy of endless youth and eternal life, the glutton need no longer fear a punitive afterlife but, rather, death itself—a premature death caused by immoderation, excess, and slovenly self-indulgence.

The superheroes of gluttony—from Gargantua to Diamond Jim Brady—have been relegated to the distant, benighted, unenlightened past. Their heirs—today's big eaters—are commonly regarded as freaks or sociopaths, or, even more commonly, as ordinary losers, misfits, unfortunate human specimens. On occasion, the hugely obese (in whom we may see frightening images of what might happen to us if we stopped heeding the promptings of social control and our own shaky superegos) are featured on the evening news, in prime-time versions of the midway side show. Often, these "news" stories concern some hapless man or woman who has grown so wide that he or she can no longer leave the house without a team of carpenters being called in to widen the doorways.

The public loves and despises the spectacle of those male and female movie stars and divas who gain and lose prodigious amounts of weight. When Liza Minnelli was married in the spring of 2002, it was widely reported that the bride had lost 90 pounds in preparation for the nuptials. These days, if you're overweight the last thing it seems to mean is that you have a passion for the tastes and flavors of food.

Yet, for all its abhorrence of tiny weight gains and minuscule accretions of body fat, the culture is fixated on identifying the trendiest restaurant and the newest exotic ingredient. What results is often the phenomenon of rich, thin, young people eating tiny and absurdly expensive portions, or worse, of young women whose understandable difficulty in interpreting the conflicting messages dispatched by the larger society contributes to the development of a host of common eating disorders. What's generally agreed upon now (at least in the popular imagination) is that the compulsive eaters, the modern-day gluttons, have some outstanding "issues" involving low self-esteem or past abuse, some bottomless void they are trying to fill by binging on massive infusions of unhealthy, fattening food.

However flawed and partial, the idea that overeating is symptomatic of a psychological disorder somehow seems (at least to the secular mind) more logical and comprehensible than the notion that gluttony should constitute a crime against the divine order. Who in the world first decided that gluttony was a *sin?* The sensible question that recurs in discussions of this particular deadly sin is: Whom exactly does it harm except the glutton himself? Admittedly, the act and the physical consequences of gluttony can be intensely unattractive, but the sin is not nearly so esthetically unappealing as, say, the more repugnant and shaming spectacles of sloth, avarice, and envy. Nor is gluttony so plainly dangerous as pride and anger, which can so easily lead to discord, violence, social chaos.

One can imagine a certain ease, a certain sureness surrounding the choices that the church fathers were obliged to make as they decided what to include on the list of the seven deadly sins. Pride and anger must have been obvious candidates. Envy and lust can wreak havoc, leaving corpses in their wake. But who, exactly, will suffer if, in that one tiny moment of self-forgetting, we help ourselves to that second or even third helping of pecan pie?

How did overeating come not merely a vice but one of the cardinal vices, with the associated reputation for corruption and contagion, a sin that leads to other sins, a gateway sin to further evil? Saint Augustine suggests—without much explanation—that gluttony leads to flattery. Possibly he is thinking of the fawning lies people tell in order to secure an invitation to a famously lavish and generous table.

For the most part, the reasoning of the early theologians concerning the contaminating nature of gluttony tends to fall into two categories, with two sets of arguments that are by no means mutually exclusive.

The first principal objection to gluttony is that worship of the senses in general and of the sense of taste in particular turns our attention from holy things and becomes a substitute for the worship of God. The phrase that recurs in sermons and warnings against gluttony is the metaphor of the belly as God, as the object of reverence and devotion. Saint Paul takes up this theme in his Epistle to the Romans (Rom. 16:17): "Now I beseech you, brethren, mark them which cause divisions and offenses contrary to the doctrine which ye have learned; and avoid them. For they that are such serve not our Lord Jesus Christ, but their own belly and by good words and fair speeches deceive the hearts of the simple." He returns to the subject in his Epistle to the Philippians (Phil. 3:18-19): "For many walk, of whom I have told you often, and now tell you even weeping, that they are the enemies of the cross of Christ. Whose end is destruction, whose God is their belly, and whose glory is in their shame, and who mind earthly things."

The second theory is that gluttony makes us let down our guard, weakens our moral defenses, and thus paves the way for lechery and debauchery, an argument that seemed especially cogent during those centuries when the term "gluttony" signified not only excessive eating (as it is mostly understood today) but also overindulgence in drink. For Saint Basil the link between gluttony and lust was fairly direct, as "through the sense of touch in tasting—which is always seducing toward gluttony by swallowing, the body, fattened up and titillated by the soft humors bubbling uncontrollably inside, is carried in a frenzy towards the touch of sexual intercourse."[3]

In arguing for the inclusion of gluttony among the deadly sins, the sins that lead to other sins, Aquinas lists the "six daughters" that overeating is likely to spawn: "excessive and unseemly joy, loutishness, uncleanness, talkativeness, and an uncomprehending dullness of mind."[4] Overindulgence, it was generally agreed, offered an open invitation to lust, anger, and sloth. In other words, the six daughters crop up in our behavior when we're drunk or stuffed with food, when we have eaten ourselves into a state of consciousness—or unconsciousness—in which we've stopped thinking rationally and have begun to act in ways that look better from the inside than the outside.

According to a popular medieval legend, the hermit John of Beverley was tested by God, who sent an angel to force John to choose among three sins: drunkenness, rape, or murder. Sensibly, as anyone might, the hermit chose drunkenness. Or not so sensibly, as it would soon turn out, because, in his drunken insensate stupor, he raped and murdered his own sister.

In Chaucer, the tale told by the vain, corrupt, proudly unrepentant, and sexually ambiguous Pardoner is, in theory, an illustration of the principle that greed (a sin with which the mercenary Pardoner is presumably acquainted on a firsthand basis) is the root of all evil. But as it happens, greed is only a sort of byproduct of the real sin at the dark heart of this tale, which, of course, is gluttony.

Part narrative, part sermon, part parody of a sermon, the Pardoner's charged, overheated rant is a haunting, spooky evocation of the daughters of gluttony, the violent and chaotic horrors to which eating and drinking can lead. In that way, it resembles the story of John of Beverley: bloody-minded evidence that the deceptively innocuous sin of gluttony is the mother of far worse evil. It functions as a sort of quick march, a breathless tour through past and popular arguments against overeating and drinking, railings from earlier centuries that were doubtless still heard, in Chaucer's era, from actual individuals more or less exactly like the Pardoner.

The Pardoner begins by describing a group of young debauchees in Flanders, heavy eaters and serious drinkers, profaners, frequenters of taverns, clients of the prostitutes and dancers who work to

> kindle and blow upon the fire of lechery
> That is attached to Gluttony.
> For the holy Scripture I take as my witness
> that lust is in wine and drunkenness.[5]

The Pardoner breaks off his narrative to call upon biblical authority. He cites the story of Lot, who drank so much that he failed to notice that he was sleeping with his own daughters, and the crime of Herod who, when drunk, allowed himself to be persuaded that John the Baptist should be beheaded. For good measure and to marshal additional evidence in support of his case, he cites the classics, tossing in Seneca's remark on how hard it is to distinguish a drunk man from a mad one.

By now the Pardoner has nearly forgotten the three revelers of Flanders, so far gone is he into the sort of preaching that would have convinced his food-and-drinking loving listeners that they desperately needed the absolution that could be purchased along with the Pardoner's holy relics. His sermon is like an aria, during which the pitch keeps rising to a series of crescendos, apostrophes, and pure imprecation:

Oh gluttony, full of cursedness
Cause of our first ruin
O root of our damnation.[6]

Soon enough, the Pardoner's rhetorical detour takes him all the way back to Adam and Eve, who lived blissfully in Paradise while they continued to fast but who were cast out for their gluttony, for eating the fruit of the forbidden tree. "O, if a man knew how many miseries followed from excess and gluttony, He would be more moderate in his diet when he sits at the table. Alas, the brief pleasure of swallowing, the tender mouth makes men— north and south, east and west—work to satisfy their gluttonous tastes for meat and drink."[7] The Pardoner quotes Saint Paul on the subject, then soars into a denunciation of the grossness of the body: "O womb, O belly, O stinking bag, filled with dung and corruption. At either end of thee, foul is the sound . . . "[8] And so the

Pardoner goes on and on, describing the typical drunkard (ugly, sour-breathed, hideous to embrace) and refusing to let up until he's reached the story of the death of Attila, who "died in his sleep with shame and dishonor, bleeding drunkenly from the nose."[9] After a brief meditation on the evils of gambling and swearing, the Pardoner returns to pick up the thread of his narrative.

The three drunkards of Flanders hear the tolling of the death knell, and, apparently too inebriated to identify the sound, they ask what it is. On being told that Death, aided by his helper, the Plague, has been making considerable headway in the neighborhood, they take a vow to find and kill Death. As they stumble along on their way they meet a mysterious old man who directs them to a tree under which, he says, they will find Death. But what they find instead are eight bushels of gold florins. They (drunkenly) decide to stay under the tree until nightfall, when they can remove the gold safely without being seen, and they send the youngest of the three revelers to town to bring back more food and drink.

While he's gone, the two left behind conspire to murder the third upon his return so there will be more gold for them—an idea that has, unfortunately, already occurred to their young friend, who returns with jugs of poisoned wine. After they kill their friend, the two remaining revelers celebrate by drinking the poisoned wine, which of course proves fatal. And so they have found Death after all, and in the process have worked their way through all the sins—anger, treachery, stupidity, pride, greed, and finally murder—that can be spawned by the deadly sin of gluttony, of drunkenness and overindulgence.

Chaucer's portrayal of the gluttons and revelers is not unlike the representation of gluttony that appears in another fourteenth-century work, William Langland's *The Vision of Piers Plowman:*

> Gluttony he gave also and great oaths together,
> All day to drink at divers taverns,
> There to jangle and jape and judge their fellow Christians.
> And on fast days to feed before the full time
> And then sit and sup till sleep them assail,
> And to breed like town swine and repose at their ease
> Till sloth and sleep make slek their sides;
> And Despair to awaken them so with no wiall to amend;
> They believe themselves loast. This is their last end.[10]

In his *Imitation of Christ*, Thomas à Kempis summed up the matter even more succinctly: "When the belly is full to bursting with food and drink, debauchery knocks at the door."[11] So naturally we cannot be mindful of God or of our final end or even of our human nature or moral responsibilities when, carried away by gluttony, we are behaving like the animal that came to symbolize the sin—that is to say, the pig.

How did the odd, long, and enduring career of gluttony make it seem so much more serious than one of those secret failings that the sinner might worry about in the quiet of the night, at that moment when one wakes consumed with regret over that extra lamb chop, the second bowl of rice pudding? How did gluttony graduate beyond the personal list of character flaws that the penitent might whisper about in the privacy of the confessional—and how did it become, as it is today, the most excruciatingly public of the sins, the nearly unforgivable crime against the self and society that, like Hester Prynne's scarlet A, is worn constantly, a badge of shame that not only brands the wrongdoer but, like the evil space creature from *Alien*, comes to inhabit the sinner's own body? How did gluttony—and the related issues of thinness, body image, weight, eating disorders, and so forth—become such a widespread and all-consuming cultural obsession that if we define sin, as a number of the church fathers did, as the cause and subject of inordinate and extreme interest and desire, then by that logic we have become a nation of gluttons, a society of sinners?

Like Chaucer's Pardoner, those who have wished to establish a lineage for gluttony, to trace its roots back to the beginnings of Judeo-Christian tradition have claimed that the urge to commit gluttony was among the promptings that tempted Adam and Eve to taste the forbidden fruit. In her thoughtful study of medieval fasting, *The Burden of the Flesh*, Teresa M. Shaw quotes the early church philosophers who—like the Pardoner—argued that if Adam had only practiced abstinence or moderation, we would all still be gamboling naked, enjoying the fruits of the garden, and naming the animals in Eden. Furthermore, the church fathers preached, those Christians who took up fasting might miraculously be granted return to the lost purity of Paradise.

This interpretation of Adam's fall is also often cited in the gluttony-leads-to-lechery arguments against excessive eating and drinking. First Adam and Eve ate the apple, then they discovered sex. Gluttony, then lust. It might be argued more logically that one bite of an apple hardly constitutes gluttonous eating or drinking, or the sort of eating orgy (such as the one portrayed in Tony Richardson's film version of *Tom Jones*) that can shift so seamlessly from the table to the bed. To not understand that Adam and Eve's sin was disobedience seems somehow to miss the point of that part of Genesis. In any case, the serious gluttons in Eden would more likely have consumed the entire *crop* of the tree of knowledge.

Preachers, theologians, and more recently the designers of Christian web sites scour the Bible for warnings against gluttonous overindulgence but fail to come up with much besides the negative reference to the drunkenness of Noah, as well as general praise for the virtues of moderation and admonitions to treat the body as the temple of the Holy Ghost. Proverbs 23:20-21 advises us: "Be not among winebibbers; among riotous eaters of flesh. For the drunkard and the glutton shall come to poverty and drowsiness shall clothe a man with rags." Yet somehow the image of winebibbers and riotous eaters of flesh fails to correspond to the sin we face, left alone with the mashed potatoes. When Deuteronomy advises that the wayward son be denounced by his parents as a drunkard and a glutton, and subsequently stoned to death by the general populace, the accusation of gluttony seems merely a fillip, an add-on to the son's real sin, which is seditiousness and disobedience—rebellion against the authority of the parents and by extension, against God.

And when Proverbs enumerates the things that God hates—a proud look, a lying tongue, hands that shed innocent blood, a heart that deviseth wicked imaginations, feet that run to mischief, a false witness, he that soweth discord among brethren—it will be noted that the glutton and the overfull stomach are nowhere among them. Ecclesiastes 10:17 warns against overindulgence: "Blessed art thou, O land, when thy king is the son of nobles, and thy princes eat in due season, for strength, and not for drunkenness!" But more common is the counsel that runs through the book like a sort of refrain (Eccles. 2:24): "There is nothing better for a man, than that he should eat and drink, and that he should make his soul enjoy good in his labor. This also I saw, that it was from the hand of God."

Indeed, most of the feasting in the Old and New Testaments is, as it should be, celebratory, unclouded by guilt, regret, or remorse. Famine was properly dreaded, banquets were held to make peace and to mark victories, to welcome guests and send guests on their way. Feasts were ordered to mark the conclusion of the seven days during which unleavened bread was to be eaten in commemoration of the exodus from Egypt; set feasts and burnt offerings were prescribed in the Book of Numbers. The story of Esther concludes with a day of feasting to celebrate the Jews' deliverance from the evil conspiracies of Haman. Isaiah describes the final feast of wines and of fat things full of marrow that will accompany our ultimate redemption.

When Jesus performs the miracle of the loaves and fishes, no one seems to have been looking on with disapproval, ready to condemn those in the crowd who might have helped themselves to extra bread and fish. In a line that would play a critical role in the church fathers' subsequent discussions of gluttony, Jesus says quite plainly that we cannot be defiled by what we eat. Quite possibly this was meant to have a political significance, to serve as a way of separating Christianity from Judaism, with its elaborate dietary laws. In any case, this passage from the Scriptures became a sort of touchstone for those who would argue that what (and by extension, how much) the good Christian put in his stomach mattered less than what he had in his soul and in his heart.

In the Greco-Roman tradition, feasting, along with drinking, was the social cement that enforced the values of the citizen and kept the state together. Good feasts and the bad feasts are recurring motifs at the center of the *Odyssey,* where it is made very clear that the worth of the host depends upon the generosity of his table. At the same time, the *Odyssey* is filled with barely encrypted warnings about the perils of excess; only after having made the Cyclops drunk and slow-witted are Odysseus and his men enabled to blind him and escape from his cave—to evade his plans to eat *them.*

Like so many of the philosophers and theologians who would come after him, Aristotle counseled moderation in eating and drinking:

> Drink or food that is above or below a certain amount destroys the health, while that which is proportionate both produces and increases and preserves it. So too is it, then, in the case of temperance and courage and the other virtues. For the man who flies from and fears everything and does not stand his ground against anything becomes a coward, and the man who fears nothing at all but goes to meet every danger becomes rash; and similarly the man who indulges in every pleasure and abstains from none becomes self-indulgent, while the man who shuns every pleasure, as boors do, becomes in a way insensible;

temperance and courage, then, are destroyed by excess and defect, and preserved by the mean.[12]

And Plutarch compares the body to a ship that must not be overloaded with food and drink, or it will founder and go under.

Such sensible warnings, apparently, failed to have much effect on celebrations staged during the heyday of the Roman Empire, when thoughtful hosts installed their infamous vomitoriums to make sure that nothing would limit the guests' capacity for enjoyment. As we shall see, such works as Petronius's *Satyricon* delight in detailing the porcine excesses to which its partygoers went and invite the reader to laugh at the ludicrously lavish meal the ex-slave Trimalchio serves his acquaintances, the huge platter arranged with dishes designed to correspond to the signs of the zodiac—the testicles and kidneys for Gemini, the lobster for Capricorn. Trimalchio sends a pack of hunting dogs tearing into the dining room as a way of introducing the pièce de résistance, the roast wild boar wearing a hat. Even if we conclude (as we're meant to) that this ridiculous feast is indicative of the same coarseness and vulgarity that makes the ex-slave take an ex-whore as his consort and hire a pretty boy to distribute bunches of grapes while singing nasal hymns to the gods of food and wine, none of us—certainly not Petronius—are ready to suggest that Trimalchio should be tortured, for time and all eternity, for the sin of encouraging his guests to eat too well and too much.

Among the early Christians' responses to the world around them was a certain righteous disgust at the decadence of the Romans' excesses. So Tertullian expressed his horror at the mass belching that soured the air at the lavish feasts, the debts incurred by the degenerate families each time they assembled for dinner. Again, ideas about diet, about abstinence and indulgence were used to draw religious-political boundaries. Much of Tertullian's impassioned and lengthy defense of fasting is based on a reading of the Bible that essentially blames many of the most serious transgressions in the Old Testament—starting with Adam's fall—on the inability of the Hebrews to control their appetites and to moderate their diets. And he (indeed, somewhat graphically) cites the basic facts of human anatomy to explicate the close relationship between gluttony and lust:

> Lust without voracity would certainly be considered a monstrous phenomenon; since these two are so united and concrete that, had there been any possibility of disjoining them, the pudenda would not have been affixed to the belly itself rather than elsewhere. Look at the body: the region of these members is one and the same. In short, the order of the vices is proportionate to the order of the members. First, the belly; and then immediately the species of all other species of lasciviousness are laid subordinately to daintiness: through love of eating, love of impurity finds passage.[13]

The essential disgust for the body that percolates up through the passage above was repeated, with variations, through the works of many of the early theologians who addressed the issue of gluttony; they would reappear, as we have already seen, in such works as "The Pardoner's Tale." John Chrysostom rather graphically identified the symptoms and signs of gluttony: "Discharge, phlegm, mucus running from the nose, hiccups, vomiting, and violent belching. . . . The increase in luxury is nothing but the increase in excrement."[14]

Too soon, too delicately, too expensively, too greedily, too much. It was gluttony's misfortune that the codifying of the virtues and vices coincided with the first flowering of the Christian monastic movement and with the simultaneous growth of the idea that the body was to be ignored, denied, despised, and even, if necessary, mortified into submission. The pleasure haters and monastery dwellers (and those whose worldview placed them squarely in both categories) naturally conspired to put gluttony on the same list as lust—two impulses that, if allowed to erupt uncontrolled, would certainly hinder the smooth operation of a very particular kind of institution. Even as the church fathers were devoting pages and hours of debate to the fine points of lust, to the delicate distinctions between sinful and pardonable ways of having sex, so the increasing hatred for human physicality naturally began to focus on eating—the other principal source of sensual pleasure.

Interestingly, the glutton never managed to inspire the same ferocity of revulsion—or for that matter, the same degree of interest—as the fornicator and the adulterer. But the saints and clerics understood that similar forces were at work, and they labored to make sure that comfort and delight should not get in the way of the austere devotions, the pure concentration that true Christians were meant to reserve for God.

According to an early biography of Francis of Assisi, the saint used ashes as a spice with which he sprinkled his food in order to destroy any hint of taste. For Augustine, the battle to subdue the urge to take delight in eating presented nowhere near the challenge of the corresponding struggle to remain chaste, and yet it posed the same problem: how to avoid the lures of enjoyment. In the tenth chapter of the *Confessions,* he begins his consideration of the sin by citing the obvious fact: that it is necessary to eat. He notes that by eating and drinking we repair our bodily decay, in a kind of daily race with Death, until inevitably Death wins, and the corruptible body is at last clothed in the raiments of the spirit that remains pure for all eternity.

Augustine speaks of food as a medicine we are required to take; but the tricky part is navigating the distance between hunger to repletion with falling, along the way, into the snare of concupiscence. The bare minimum necessary for health is—as Augustine remarks and as every dieter knows—often too little for pleasure. The saint takes pride in the fact that he is not tempted to drink too much, so that refraining from drunkenness represents a far less costly victory than the triumph over the siren song of food. He cites exemplary cases as a way of distinguishing between those instances in which gluttony did, and did not, lead to other sins. Citing Noah, who after the flood was permitted to eat any flesh that could possibly be eaten, and John the Baptist surviving on locusts in the wilderness, Augustine points out that these were obviously very different situations than that of Esau, who sold his birthright for a mess of porridge. John the Baptist's unusual dietary preference was nowhere near as reprehensible as the sin of the Hebrews, who, while wandering in the desert, committed the ultimate evil of being so concerned with their bellies that it turned them away from God.

"But full feeding," the saint writes, endearingly, "sometime creepeth upon thy servant."[15] It is, as Augustine well understands, a common enough failing: Who, Lord, he asks, has not been tempted to eat a little more than he needs? He makes the distinction that began with Christ himself and reached its height with Aquinas: that what truly matters is not what one eats but the spirit and the manner in which one eats it. It's a distinction he expounds upon further in *On Christian Doctrine*:

For it is possible that a wise man may use the daintiest food without any sin of epicurism or gluttony, while a fool will crave for the vilest food with a most disgusting eagerness of appetite. And any sane man would prefer eating fish after the manner of our Lord, to eating lentils after the manner of Esau, or barley after the manner of oxen. For there are several beasts that feed on commoner kinds of food, but it does not follow that they are more temperate than we are. For in all matters of this kind it is not the nature of the things we use, but our reason for using them, and our manner of seeking them, that make what we do either praiseworthy or blameable.[16]

"I fear not the uncleanness of meat," Augustine notes in the *Confessions,* "but the uncleanness of desire."[17]

Too soon, too delicately, too expensively, too greedily, too much. Is the sin of gluttony really only an offense against the self and the body— or can it also constitute a wrong against society? In search of an answer perhaps we should turn from Augustine's confession (or *testimony,* as Garry Wills more accurately terms it in his recent biography of the saint) to my own.

How often the modern confession takes the form of the account of one's most embarrassing moment, told and retold